Through the Oak Tree

Through the Oak Tree

Poems by

Susan Gerardi Bello

© 2019 Susan Gerardi Bello. All rights reserved.
This material may not be reproduced in any form, published,
reprinted, recorded, performed, broadcast,
rewritten or redistributed without
the explicit permission of Susan Gerardi Bello.
All such actions are strictly prohibited by law.

Cover design: Shay Culligan

ISBN: 978-1-950462-37-7

Kelsay Books Inc.

kelsaybooks.com

502 S 1040 E, A119
American Fork, Utah 84003

For Angelo and Tony

Acknowledgments

The author gratefully acknowledges the following journals and websites where these poems were first published, some in a slightly different form.

Brevitas: "Asphalt," "Flowers," "Holding On," "Lessons," "Wanting"

Delaware Poetry Review: "Prince was our Elvis"

In Our Own Words: "Boys Dressed as Men"

Italian American Writers: "Confession"

Mom Egg Review: "The Language of Surrender"

Paterson Literary Review: "Baby Boomer," "Boys Dressed as Men," "Impulse," "Prom"

Schuylkill Valley Journal: "Advent," "Janis Joplin as Postage Stamp"

U.S. 1 Worksheets: "The Circle of Beasts," "Huck," "Kansas," "Porn among the Pawpaws," "The Second Day of His Birth," "Senior Year Goddesses," "War Paint"

Contents

Part I: Porn among the Pawpaws

Catechism	15
Sixth Grade Rallying Cry	16
Porn among the Pawpaws	17
Anthem	18
Backpack	19
Musical Chairs	20
Phys Ed	21
Free Bird	22
Senior Year Goddesses	23
Prince was Our Elvis	24
War Paint	25
Climbing the Gunks	26
Baby Boomer	27
I want it to be like this	28
Holding On	29

Part II: Janis Joplin as Postage Stamp

Tree,	33
Peacetime, 1989	34
Huck	35
Janis Joplin as Postage Stamp	36
Cigarettes with Angelo	37
Kansas	38
Utah	39
Dig Site	40
Advent	41
Dinner in Tahoe	42
Wanting	43

The Boy with the Bloated Belly	44
Remember the Drills?	45
Boys Dressed as Men	46
Confession	47

Part III: Lessons

The Language of Surrender	51
The Second Day of His Birth	52
Flowers	53
Clipping the Hedges	54
Choice	55
Asphalt	56
Impulse	57
Ginsberg Does the Laundry	58
Lessons	59
Prom	60
Directions for My Son	61
The Circle of Beasts	62

People talk about how wonderful the world seems to children, and that's true enough. But children think they will grow into it and understand it, and I know very well that I will not, and would not if I had a dozen lives.
—Marilynne Robinson, Gilead

Part I

Porn among the Pawpaws

Catechism

I believed what I was taught
on Saturday mornings:
If I had enough faith in God,
I could do anything.

That's what I was thinking
on my way home from class
when I tried to walk
through an oak tree.

I remember how the bark
felt hitting my nose,
rough, sharp
against my lips.

The gritty taste
familiar now
after so many years
trying and failing.

Sixth Grade Rallying Cry

During classroom recess when it was too cold
to be outside, we were allowed to play our 45s
on the record player while our teacher
was having his lunch or wandering the halls
looking for flirt-time with Mrs. D.

We played The Devil Went Down to Georgia
over and over. The fiddle got us going, that foreign, exotic
sound, nothing like the Sinatra our parents listened to,
and Johnny's arrogance, thumbing his nose
at the Devil and God. In a state of abandon,
clutching the communion crosses that hung around
our tender necks, we sang along, waiting for the moment
we could shout, *Son of a Bitch, I'm the best there's ever been!*

And we were transformed from Long Island school kids,
descendants of Italians with thick accents
to true Americans, as if we'd been here for hundreds
of years, as if the fiddle's twang belonged to us.
We gloried in the sound of it echoing off the pink cement walls.
We were sons and daughters of the American Revolution!

Porn among the Pawpaws

It was our only piece of land not chain-linked around a yard.
We raced our bikes through its trails, jumped hills
like Evel Knievel. We smoked hollow sticks,
pretended they were cigarettes, coughed from the bitter heat.

Near a fire pit built by the older kids, we discovered them
buried among empty beer bottles and cigarette butts. We thought
they were Playboys, those glossy pages we'd found hidden
in our brothers' rooms with perfect women perched on satin.

But we were wrong. They were cheap, corner-store rags
filled with harshly-lit close-ups, whole pages of hairy parts
alone and stuck together, grotesque reminders
of how our bodies were changing.

We stared at them, the same way we stared when a rock
was lifted and the bugs underneath squirmed in the light.
Through the treetops the sun shimmered down on us,
the smell of leaf mold and ashes in the air.

Anthem

Only Led Zeppelin can scream me back
to late afternoons on hot school rooftops.
Black tar stain on cut-off short shorts,
cigarette at lips and corrupt company
with his own set of wheels, two with broken spokes.
I would balance on the back, holding his tiny waist,
pulling his bony frame against my flat chest.
Rebel virgins, neither of us boy or girl
but thinking we were so distinctly our sex;
we bragged of blowjobs and fingerjobs
like we'd given or gotten them.
And all the while, from a banged-up radio
strapped to the handle bars
Robert Plant screamed our anthem.

Backpack

A week into the new school year, on my way home,
I saw his books and papers strewn across the cement
playground. I didn't know if someone had pushed them
down or if he had dropped them. I helped him
pick them up. When I got home, I asked my mother if we
could get him a backpack, but she had already gotten
the four of us one, plus school supplies, new clothes.
She said I could bring him a paper bag. I did.
But I wish it had been a backpack, a cool one
that would leave his hands free to run away
or punch the bully in the face.

Musical Chairs

First by one, then picked up by the crowd,
the whole class chants his name,
Brayden, Brayden, Brayden!

His opponent hears no cheers of her own. Toothless mouth
gaping, in tutu and chocolate-stained top, she frowns
at the last chair. He is at ease, smiling.

The chants quicken, become louder.
The play button is pressed; they scuttle 'round the chair.
I close my eyes, press stop. Frenzied cheers, victory again.

See them all, out there, on the sand of that wild shore, dirt
on their faces. See how they dance 'round the pig's head
on its wooden stake. *Brayden, Brayden, Brayden!*

Phys Ed

No matter how quickly we changed our clothes
or how slyly the gym shirt was pulled
over and under and up, everyone could see.

We were flat-chested except for one girl.
We regarded her as slutty not because she was
but because she looked like she was.

We told each other she was deformed.
Her chest just looked big because she had
an abnormally sunken breastplate.

We envied those full, swaying breasts,
so soft and new. We wanted to touch them.
It was hard not to stare, not to imagine

how they might feel resting against our cheeks
or pressed against our lips.

Free Bird

The song blared from the speakers at the Junior Prom,
an abrupt change from the 80s New Wave
that had played all night. We outsiders stopped
to listen, to look at the table where her friends sat,
some of the girls crying, holding each other,
the boys staring. The cool table had lost one
of their own, the coolest girl, to alcohol
poisoning. At least that's the story that went around
the hallways. She had blacked out one night, months before
on the football field, had to have her stomach pumped.
But this time, she wasn't coming back
with her Farrah Fawcett hair, her raspy
27-year-old voice. I had wanted to be her,
but my curls could never manage those wings.
We heard she was buried in her prom dress,
probably nothing like my predictable pink.
Maybe she wore white, her perfectly waved
brown hair resting on her shoulders.

Senior Year Goddesses

We changed in the dark basement, surrounded
by taxidermy. There were side tables with furry
legs, hoof ashtrays, deer and pheasant judging us
from the walls. We slipped our milky bodies
into swimsuits, we were lights shining
on the dead beasts. Who dusted them?
I wondered, were they vacuumed, brushed?
We tossed our curly hair, a set of triplets
from different parents. We pulled at our suits,
forever self-conscious, though it was only the three of us,
and the brown eyes watching. Their unblinking lashes
more lush than our own. We stole away
from their stare through the sliding doors
to the back patio, eased our way into the pool.
The Smiths lamented from a cassette player:
It's not natural, normal or kind, the flesh
you so fancifully fry. We made a pact
to be vegetarians, one of the many pacts
we made that year. Our dreams more real
than the feel of our skin moving through the water.

Prince was Our Elvis

I remember my mother's reaction when Elvis died: tears,
of course, and a phone call to our next-door neighbor Mrs. Laurel.
The two of them on the phone crying, my mother stretching
the long yellow telephone cord all the way to the back door
to see Mrs. Laurel who was also looking out her back door.

For us it was text messages, Twitter, Facebook posts.
If it's not online it hasn't really happened, so we google
to confirm, and the list comes down: *Prince is Dead, Prince Death,
Prince Dies at 57*. Now we know and we weep, yes for his music,
his genius, but mostly we weep for ourselves, for those awkward
teenagers who listened to his every word with wonder and shock,
and through him learned about living with abandon:
Strip right down to your underwear.

We imagined ourselves in our cotton panties
and JCPenney bras on a dance floor next to him
letting go of all we were supposed to be, all we hoped to be,
just being who we were—young and beautiful with rock-solid
bodies, abounding energy, and the will to keep moving
until the sweat poured off us. He never stopped
and we never stopped, we were everything
and he wrote us that way and we believed him.

War Paint

We gathered in front of the dimly lit bathroom mirror.
The pink tiled walls made our reflections glow,
made us look more beautiful than we already were.
But we didn't see those flawless nymphs looking back at us,
we saw only a large nose, a pimple, flat hair.
One of us would take out the forbidden matches.
We fumbled through our purses, finding our stubs of eyeliner
and held them to the flame. We were careful to test
the tip with a finger before applying under our eyes.
With our armor in place, we made one final look
at ourselves, fingering our hair, worthy now,
we thought, to step out into the hallway,
to the bright fluorescents where the boys waited.

Climbing the Gunks

Shawangunk Mountains, NY

She kills another Saturday trying to find herself,
clutches an old Othello paperback,
wanders to the bridge in bargain-store sneakers,
peers over the edge where she spots Dylan.
He drives them to the Gunks
in his rust-bottomed Nova.

With his crooked-tooth smile, he suggests they climb.
Sneaker, rock. Up. Hand, rock. Up.
He rises ahead, shows her the good places to step.

When they reach the top, they get high on Dylan's weed,
bask in the view as the sun starts to dip, and the sky turns red.

With bravado she takes the lead on the way down.

As she places her tread-bare sole on an unseen patch
of moss, she slips and slides down. Her breasts
and stomach scrape along the rock. Clouded brain
pulls into focus, and she just misses falling
into a crevice below.

He calls out to her as she lands on a ledge, inches
from the opening, her name echoes off the mountains.

Baby Boomer

You brought your guitar to 4th of July picnics.
I was love-struck watching you strum,
your longish hair touching your ears.
You were the quiet rebel,
the hitchhiker, rarely home.
We were told you hitchhiked to Hawaii.
I imagined you with a thumb out
on a runway in California.
Your brothers who stayed
drank too much, snorted too much,
got arrested. But not you, cousin.
You survived, even that fall
from forty stories.
I remember smoking cigarettes with you
on the back steps of the summerhouse.
Me on break from college, you it seemed
always on break from something.
We talked; the others were out fishing.
You spoke softly of uncertainty and freedom.
You didn't call it freedom
but I knew that's what it was.

I want it to be like this

for Angelo

It's a perfect summer day, hot but not humid.
I am walking down the streets of Carroll Gardens,
he is sitting on the porch waiting for me, smoking,
listening to birds. I walk up and he smiles, doesn't look
at my body despite the fact it is prominently displayed.
He offers me a smoke, lights it for me. I study his face,
the warm brown eyes, fine hairs on his cheekbones,
the way his hand brushes aside his thick hair. I want
to tell him what I see, but I don't, I just smoke.
We talk about family, faith, art, New York.
I'm surprised I can manage words at all. I wish
only my heart would speak, tentative, stuttering,
sincere in its confusion, half believing in love.

Holding On

They walk over from the pool, flip-flops flapping,
damp bathing suits underneath short-shorts and t-shirts,
and in one case, silky black cover-up, a little too formal,
and a little too black for a playground. They are clearly
past the playground's recommended age. Their legs
are lean and muscular, inner thighs taut when they stretch
to sit in the wooden car, absent-mindedly turn the wheel.
They wander through the playground, one of them exclaims,
Where's the tire swing? They are too young for nostalgia,
yet why else have they come if not to remember,
to retreat to this place where as little girls
they laughed, held onto chain-link, kicked
at the ground to move the giant tire, wild and jerky,
ponytails flying.

Part II

Janis Joplin as Postage Stamp

Tree,

with the giant hole down the middle
of your massive trunk, how you survive,
rising the way you do, branches healthy,
arms extended for the sun. You live in the sky,
not in your wound. Do you even remember it?
You seem so unaware, the way it can rot inside.
Oh, to be like you, tree! Of the earth, the dark,
but soaring above in the light. You are braver than I.
Teach me.

Peacetime, 1989

We lived privileged and warless with our meal plans
and geometric haircuts. What were we united for?
Against? Nothing. We were concerned only for ourselves.
We bought Nag Champa at the used book store on Main
as if the incense would connect us to that other generation.
And it did somehow, the way it smoldered, smoked up a room,
sneaked under the door to disturb the dormmates.
Not sweet-smelling apple or peach, bought by girls
who didn't know better, but a dense, nearly choking
sandalwood, an earthy call-to-action—but to where, what, when?
I pulled on layers: sweater, boots, second-hand coat,
headed out in the cold air, hoping to find something,
toes frozen minutes after leaving, at least that was a feeling
that hurt. I walked across campus, over the stone bridge,
through the order to the open field, expansive,
nestled by woods all around. It was something to be there,
where it was rumored something had happened,
students had gathered, to listen to music, protest a war.

I imagined all those feet pressing on the grass,
bending it down, pressure, ground, purpose.
I envied a war, decided to grow my hair, stood there
breathing the cold Catskills' air when I heard him singing.
He came from the woods full voice, *Wild, wild horses...*
When he saw me, he stopped. We knew each other
from English Lit, the only two who ever asked questions.
He walked over and we talked until the sun fell
behind the trees, until there was nothing left to say—
we made love on the frozen ground.

Huck

How could I be coming to him so late?
Who should I blame? The public schools?
Afraid to let us study a book with that word in it?
Myself? Obsessed always with the others:
Anna Karenina, Emma, needing to know
what the deal was with Prufrock.
The language fit like a crinoline underneath
all that fancy silk and lace,
and though scratchy, it was very good.

Then there's Huck. Simple cotton,
holes in the elbows and knees,
feet cold, socks that need mending.
Finally, home with him, a survivor I know,
but still, another abused child. Would he let me
hold him, allow a mother's comfort?
It doesn't matter, the book is solid,
the spine glued, he is my child
for these 336 pages, and I am holding him now.

Janis Joplin as Postage Stamp

If you knew at 27 that your suffering would come to this—
a 49-cent postage stamp—what would you say?
What would you scream into the microphone
these many years later, your body rotten,
yet your young, unblemished face preserved
in glossy color, eyes shining with hope, that smile—
a smile that makes me want to run with you,
climb on that freight car, rest my back against
rumbling steel and listen to your voice
more powerful than the train wheels scraping
against the metal track, how you cut through it all
with that soul-cry, that wish to be heard. Beauty
unhinged and ephemeral like Virginia bluebells
in soggy earth, how they sing their color, pink turning
to blues, blues that surprise in the dark green forest,
the tall oaks blocking out much of the sun, sharing very little
with the bells below, but they don't need much light,
do they, Janis, to clang, to make themselves known.
If only you could do what the bluebells do
and resurrect every spring.

Cigarettes with Angelo

You hand me one, stand to get the lighter,
don't sit back down. I ask if you'll join me,
I watch the decision move across your face.

On the bench in the sun,
you tell me I look nice.
A warm breeze, I inhale,
smoke three in a row.

Cigarettes. All those years I kept them around
when everyone said no good could come of them.

Kansas

For Joe and Tammy

We drove with only the cow grates to upset the rhythm
and even they became normal to us after a while.
There was nothing to see but land and sky in any direction.
Land, sky, and cows.

We stopped for lunch, ate chunks of beef served over lettuce
in little baskets. The beef was a cliché, melting in our mouths
like a tab of butter on a warm skillet, and it was cheap, and better
than any steak we'd ever had in New York. We joked how
the cows had probably walked over to the kitchen that morning.

After lunch, we took to the road again—the plain flatness
a friend now—respected for what it yields. Then sunset came
all at once; like a bomb it blasted its light across the land.
No, not a bomb—a soul-kiss, making the whole body
of the land respond with waves of color, receiving and receiving.

What could we say after the sun fell, knowing this happens
every day here—earth and sky lovemaking. I could almost believe
the earth was flat, that it had an edge, and if I went too far,
I would fall off.

Utah

The drab Nevada landscape gave way
to bursts of orange, red-brown.
Gray. Brown. Gray. Red-brown. Orange. Red.
Red-orange velvet cake, layer upon layer,
rock and clay, whatever it was until we had to
stop, pull over roadside and look and look like inmates
who'd just seen real color for the first time.
What did we know of it, except for the Crayola lines
we'd drawn as kids. Perhaps some fall leaves
we'd collected, but never an entire landscape.
My brother grabbed his camera, snapped and snapped.
I stood there, owl-eyed, wishing red-orange
would travel through my eyes to my heart,
keep that stubborn thing beating.

Dig Site

There are bits of me scattered over vast amounts of land,
difficult to get to, the once-soft me fused to rock.

To find me, to see me wholly, one must take care
with a chisel and tap, tap, tap. There it is, a little bit of me,
sort of beautiful once cleared, and polished, held to the light.

There are other pieces easier to unearth, but harder to find,
buried deep and far from the rock. Baffling
how one could be separated from oneself by so much space,
little or no pattern to explain it.

It is the finding that is difficult, but I am hopeful.
Beneath it all, cool clay sandy loam, I will be found.
I know this because I am the pieces and I am the digger.

Advent

This morning I break new ice,
sink to the bottom of winter's pond.

I am told there should be sunlight and dreaming,
and the will to push on, fueled by light.

Where is it now, stuck here as I am, in darkness
with suspended bluegills and sleeping frogs?

Light reaches through, they say, even heat.
See the algae, the green curling things, proof.

Endure the bottom, they say, keep company
with the whirligig beetles, the cold slowing of the heart.

Dinner in Tahoe

Over bacon-wrapped prawns she tells
of her childhood, moved from foster home
to foster home, how she had to bathe in a bucket
in the kitchen because she was not allowed to use
the bathroom tub, how she fought to keep
her younger sister with her—and succeeded.
She was proud of that, I could see.

And now we are here in this fancy restaurant
with white tablecloths and expensive wine.
She is waited on, napkin placed in her lap,
the bacon crisp. The prawns snap when bitten.

Wanting

The unkempt one-bedroom house struggles
to be a home without a woman, the soft, flowered details
absent, an abundance of brown furniture, frayed
kitchen towels. The only comfort a widower can offer
his children is fried bacon, nearly every morning
and sometimes at night with dinner.
The children take up those crisp offerings,
grind them with new molars.
There is something like mother in the salt and fat.

The Boy with the Bloated Belly

We are in elementary school having lunch
in the cafeteria; peanut butter and jelly, pickles,
egg salad. *Who brought that? What a stink!*
We compare desserts: raisins versus chocolate
chip cookies. These are the things we notice.
And him. That little boy who looks like
he is in first grade, but is in fourth. So small
with a belly so large. We watch him pick
through the garbage cans. *Eww, what is he doing?
What is he looking for?*

Remember the Drills?

Most of us knew they wouldn't save us, especially
those of us with an older sister who had nightmares
about the bomb. Dad tried to calm her down when
she couldn't sleep, but how calm can anyone be
with the constant threat of nukes from the Russians?

Still, we crouched under our desks or against the hallway
wall, hands holding our heads. For our teachers, our parents,
but we knew the truth—how our clothes would burn
to our skin, our hair torched in seconds.

Boys Dressed as Men

I am not done mourning

the boys dressed as men
in their charcoal grey and black business suits.
Some wearing them well, some better off in jeans,
a tee shirt, sweats, and a cap.

Boys who would check themselves out
in the windows of buildings
on their way to work.
Some stealing an awkward side glance,
others staring themselves right in the eye
and nodding their heads in approval.

Self-proclaimed knights of New York,
men of thirty-two
but boys really.

Boys who played baseball in Central Park after work
or ran hoops at the local gym.
Boys who met me at happy hour and made me laugh,
not afraid of telling it like it is,
of being too loud or out of line.

Boys dressed as men whose final moments
were spent standing in broken windows,
clinging to the walls of a building that would betray them.
Side by side like so many days at work,

and so many nights at play,
staring out at a city unable to save them,
a city aching to embrace them.

I am not done mourning.

Confession

I wasn't here. I was asleep
in an apartment in Santa Monica.

I saw it on TV, didn't smell the smoke,
flee over the bridge. I moved back a year later,

rented a row house in Brooklyn
from a man who lost his son in the North Tower.

When I moved in, I was told his son had lived
in the same house with friends, had stained

the dark wood in the living room. I was told
I could paint anything, except that dark wood.

Some nights when it was late, and I climbed
the creaky stairs to bed, I'd listen for his son,

but all I ever heard were my feet on the floorboards.

Part III

Lessons

The Language of Surrender

> *slowly alone in the center of a circle I have*
> *passed the new person out*
>   —Sharon Olds

I have not passed the new person out slowly,
alone in the center of a circle. No, I did not shake
and sweat, though I did feel the stabbing pain, briefly,
the quick onset of Pitocin. Still it was not enough
to make the boy inch down the entryway.

The boy does not like the contractions, my doctor said
and I was offering him only a centimeter of greeting.
She calmly added, *I need to take this baby out.*
And I said, *Sure, take him, take him out.*

I did little, sat upright, curved my spine, allowed
the needle to pass between the vertebrae.

In the operating room, arms strapped down at my sides,
the blue sheet raised, I trusted not my body but the woman
who was cutting me open, reaching inside to get the boy.

I heard her say, *Oh, that's why he didn't like the contractions.*
She unwrapped the cord from around his neck,
and then again, *That's why.* His feet too were wrapped.

After he was out and breathing, they brought him to me
on my side of the sheet. I welcomed him with my voice,
my face, his body pressed to my cheek, my arms still tied
down while I was closed, sewn and stapled.

The Second Day of His Birth

St. Luke's-Roosevelt, New York City

Remember when I said to you, *Hold your son.*
And you said, *Later.* And I said, *You didn't hold him
yesterday. Hold your son now.* I knew you were afraid,
but you took him from me, and held him.
I watched you feel the smallness, saw the terror
when you realized how light he was, lighter than
the wood logs you split, the shovelsful of soil
you turned over in your father's garden,
all the labor a son does when a father demands it—
pouring cement, stacking wood, burying fig trees.
The lightest thing you held was the bird in your arms
just before you killed it. Light, dumb chicken,
so easy to chop off its head, three pounds
heavier than your two-day old son.

Flowers

I need to consult with them when the demons come
to help ward off the knocking of the sticks against the trunk.
Wherever there is open ground, I plant them.
Manic I dig without gloves, my hands ground-in-green
for weeks. I bed them while my child cries in the stroller
parked on the grass. I'm not mother, nor wife, nor daughter,
nor friend. I am nothing but thirsty roots and worm castings.

Clipping the Hedges

He hung in the Snugli against my body
asleep while I hacked the thorny hedges
with a long clipper. His legs the same size
as the bigger branches which required
several cuts of the dull blade. His arms
like the smaller limbs, one strong slice
took care of those. It was madness, I knew
as I thrust his sleeping body forward
toward the sharp thorns. He slept
through it all. Later, when he was awake
cooing at me, I saw the red scratches
along his baby-fat arms and legs,
I wished I could blame the thorns.

Choice

I don't know if he'll understand when he's older.
My decision to have one, him. My choice
not to try, not to surrender to fate, or science
or whatever it is—God? I have studied
the lesson of the tree and the fruit and the snake—
never knowing the right and wrong of it.
There is just our son, his voice echoing in the halls
of this too-big house. What can I offer in response,
but my own voice singing back. He is what I have
chosen, and he is song enough for me.

Asphalt

When they are born, they are like pavement millers
preparing the way for new asphalt, scraping off the old
down to the subgrade, tearing it to shreds, making mother
raw so they can make her new. She will never be
the same, all her experiences will be changed,
pain and victories that once marked the way
will be smoothed over by what has come—
infant, real and semi-permanent like miles of new road.
Without markers to distinguish direction, purpose, effect—
moving forward is an act of faith.

Impulse

My arm has risen, my hand has opened
to slap. I did not slap, but pulled my hand
down. My son has seen this violent gesture,
knowing what my hand might do
if the impulse continued unhindered,
pushed through like the swing of a racket.
There was a look in his eyes, not fear,
but anticipation, glee. I must have worn
the same expression when my father
drew his hand. Was it my lack of fear
that pushed him to continue his swing?
Was it the same look that left my son's cheek
untouched, my hand cowering in my lap?

Ginsberg Does the Laundry

He showed up one day through the open door on the back porch,
tracking in grass from the mowed lawn, fall leaves in his hair.
He walked toward me, cheeks ruddy from the cool air,
took the towel from my hands and folded it,
placed it down on the dryer top, grabbed another,
did the same until they were all folded,
even the little washcloths my son uses. He paused
at these, the size of them seemed to amuse him.
Then he glanced down at the pile in front of the washer,
men's shirts, socks, boy's shorts, underwear.
He delighted in this pile, sprayed OxiClean on the shirt collars,
rubbed it in hard. Then he pushed the *on* button, poured
detergent in, loaded the clothes. I moved to help him,
but he wanted to do it all himself, to savor each dirty sock.

Lessons

My son and I shower—
the only way to get him to bathe
in his tub-phobia phase.
He likes to hold the showerhead.
I encourage him to spray me in the face.
I want to show him
water in the face isn't so bad.
See, it's fun!
And it is, one, two, three times.
But when the water fills
my mouth and nose
again and again,
it feels like drowning.
I think of waterboarding
as my son laughs,
holds the stream to my face.

Prom

If I had a girl and she was going to prom,
we would buy a discount dress in a pretty color,
stockings and make-up at CVS,
hair at home in front of the bathroom mirror.

We would talk about what could happen,
but wouldn't. I would tell her that I liked the boy,
but boys are boys and will be boys
though I wouldn't say it that way.

The boy would not drive, his parents would hire
a car service. I would expect a corsage,
preferably for the wrist. There would be a curfew,
no later than eleven. The boy would be a gentleman

as he promised when my husband took him aside
to remind the boy he was taking our daughter
to the prom. But I do not have a girl,
I have a boy. I can see him holding the corsage.

I do not know whether his hand will tremble
when he slides the flowers on her wrist
or if he will be steady, fingers firm
as he pushes the elastic along her hand.

Directions for My Son

When I die, don't have them put paste on my face,
don't worry about my hair, or how to dress me,
don't pay any mind to my body, that way
you won't be compelled to kiss my face,
to feel death on your lips. Have me burned,

take what remains and let me go where life is—
in the compost pile Dad built. Did you know
that it's okay for palms from Palm Sunday
to be placed there too? So don't feel bad
about doing the same to me.

But if the compost is too close, place me
on the slope off the Azalea Trail at Bowman's
where we explored together, your little feet
walking ahead, the woods entirely yours.
Remember the spider webs, and the mayapples,
the Sassafras leaves shaped like mittens?

Save the rest of me, two hands full, and take me
with you on a boat to the Shinnecock Inlet.
You don't know this place but I want you to.
Release what's left of me there.
I hope this wish of mine doesn't hurt you.
But it will, won't it? No getting around that.
Still I'd rather you mourn with salt spray in your face,
the sound of water lapping at the boat.

The Circle of Beasts

Grounds for Sculpture, Hamilton, NJ

Reflections on Dana Stewart

We are at the circle of beasts.
My son asks, *What's that? What's that?*
He likes the look of them.
I tell him:
Howling Beast,
Lamenting Beast.
He shouts the names,
likes the sound of them.
He runs, points, asks, repeats.
I try to explain to him
what lamenting means:
Like sadness, I say, *but more*
than sadness.
He moves quickly to Sue's Nightmare,
has forgotten lamenting
but I have not. I can think of nothing else
as I look at my nightmare,
imagine it, imagine my son in it.
He laughs; the beasts are toys.
I join him in his laughter,
try to fear a little less
but I know I am part of this circle.
And so is he.

About the Author

Susan Geradi Bello lives with her husband and son in Bucks County, PA. She is a member of the U.S. 1 Poets Cooperative in Princeton, NJ, and for three years served as selecting editor for their journal U.S. 1 Worksheets. Susan currently co-hosts the Bucks County Bards monthly poetry series at The Newtown Library Company, and is a member of the online, short poetry collective Brevitas. She has been published in journals in print and online, including *Mom Egg Review, New Verse News, Paterson Literary Review,* and *Schuylkill Valley Journal.* Susan is a two-time Pushcart Prize nominee. She can be reached at susangerardi@hotmail.com.